WHERE THE LOVE IS

Where The Love Is

POEMS BY

David Thompson

THE HOBNOB PRESS
2023

First published in the United Kingdom in 2023 by

The Hobnob Press,
8 Lock Warehouse, Severn Road, Gloucester GL1 2GA
www.hobnobpress.co.uk

© David H. Thompson text and images, 2023

The Author hereby asserts his moral rights to be identified as the Author of the Work.

All rights reserved. No part of this publication may be reproduced, stored in a retrieval system, or transmitted in any form or by any means, electronic, mechanical, photocopying, recording or otherwise, without the prior permission of the publisher and copyright holder.

British Library Cataloguing in Publication Data
A catalogue record for this book is available from the British Library

ISBN 978-1-914407-48-2

Typeset in Adobe Garamond Pro 12/14 pt.
Typesetting and origination by John Chandler

For Tom, Jess, Joe, Charlotte, Freya and Sienna

> Let me sometimes dance
> With you,
> Or climb
> Or stand perchance
> In ecstasy,
> Fixed and free
> In a rhyme,
> As poets do.
>
> Edward Thomas, from *Words*

Acknowledgements

Versions of several of these poems have appeared in the social media pages of Frome's Words at the Black Swan. 'An Afternoon Walk in the Jura', a finalist in the 'Walking Home' competition run by Walk.Listen.Create in spring 2022, was published in the resulting anthology, while 'Rock Pools on the Tide Line' won the Gower Walking Festival's creative writing prize in September 2022. Both appeared in print and as recordings on the Walk.Listen.Create website. 'Language Love' was published on the Autumn Voices website after winning the flash competition in February 2022. 'Running Out Of Time' appeared in *Sparks*, a compilation of poems concerned with climate change following a series of Hot Poets workshops in early 2022.

I've much enjoyed the Spring 2022 Word/Play workshops arranged by Katy Tilley of Take Art and led by Liv Torc and Jon Seagrave in Somerset; the ekphrastic poetry sessions arranged by Crysse Morrison and then by Mike Grenville in conjunction with exhibitions at the Black Swan Arts Centre in Frome; and the Forsaking the Mic poetry group on Zoom led by Tim King.

Once again, I'm especially grateful to two exceptional writers who have offered generous encouragement. Claire Crowther has continued my education as a poet by example and with perceptive comments and judicious advice, while Crysse Morrison gave constant support and inspiration from her skill and rich experience as a fiction and drama writer, poet and critic.

My children – Daniel, Charis and Matthew Thompson – have again backed me in every endeavour, however unlikely. Thank you.

PROLOGUE

Where The Love Is

Hand in hand along the dunes,
bent into the wind,
laughing to see the white horses
gallop to catch the waves
in the gathering storm.

Then home through the woods,
past the fox's lair
and a second sea, of sunflowers,
glimpses of vanishing deer,
hawks overhead,
to where the love is.

Contents

PROLOGUE
Where The Love Is   8

I MEMORY

Blackberry Picking	14
Hedging with Jack	15
Love Note to the Rock Under the Bridge	16
Take Me Away	17
Snake	18
The First Dance	19
A Swim in the Wet	20
Rock Pools on the Tide Line	21
An Afternoon Walk in the Jura	22

II LOVING

Prose Poem	26
You Are My Light	27
When We Last Met	28
Narcissus in Arcadia: A True Romance	29
A Different Silence	30
Living with Dying	31
Absence	33
If My Heart	34
Totem	35

Love: A Dual Acrostic	36
Porcelain Heart	37

III THE WAY THINGS ARE

How Was Your Year?	40
Sorting Pockets	41
Fruit Salad	42
Enough	43
Languages Like These	44
Retrograding	45
Resculpting	47
Retreat from the Edge	49

IV ECOSYSTEMS

Winning the Race to Zero	52
Running Out Of Time	54
Together	55

V GARDENS

February Storm	58
Modest Winter	59
Forgiving the Judas Tree	60
Painting the Ginkgo	61
Sightlines	62
Time Out of War	63
Mousetrap	64
Red Admiral	65
Autumn Wind-Down	66

VI GALLERY VOICES

Pinhole	70
Iterations	71
A Duet of Lines	72
Stump in Wartime	73
The Life of Rocks	74
Shortcut to Provence	75
Girl with the Square Helmet	76

VII ENCOUNTERS

Promise the Earth	80
Minor Operation	81
Taxi	82
Climbing the Kerb	83

VIII SONGS AND STORIES

Sharing: The Animals' Welcome Carol	86
Happy New Year!	87
Three Hometown Clerihews	88
Never	89
Let's Call It A Day	90
Everlasting	92

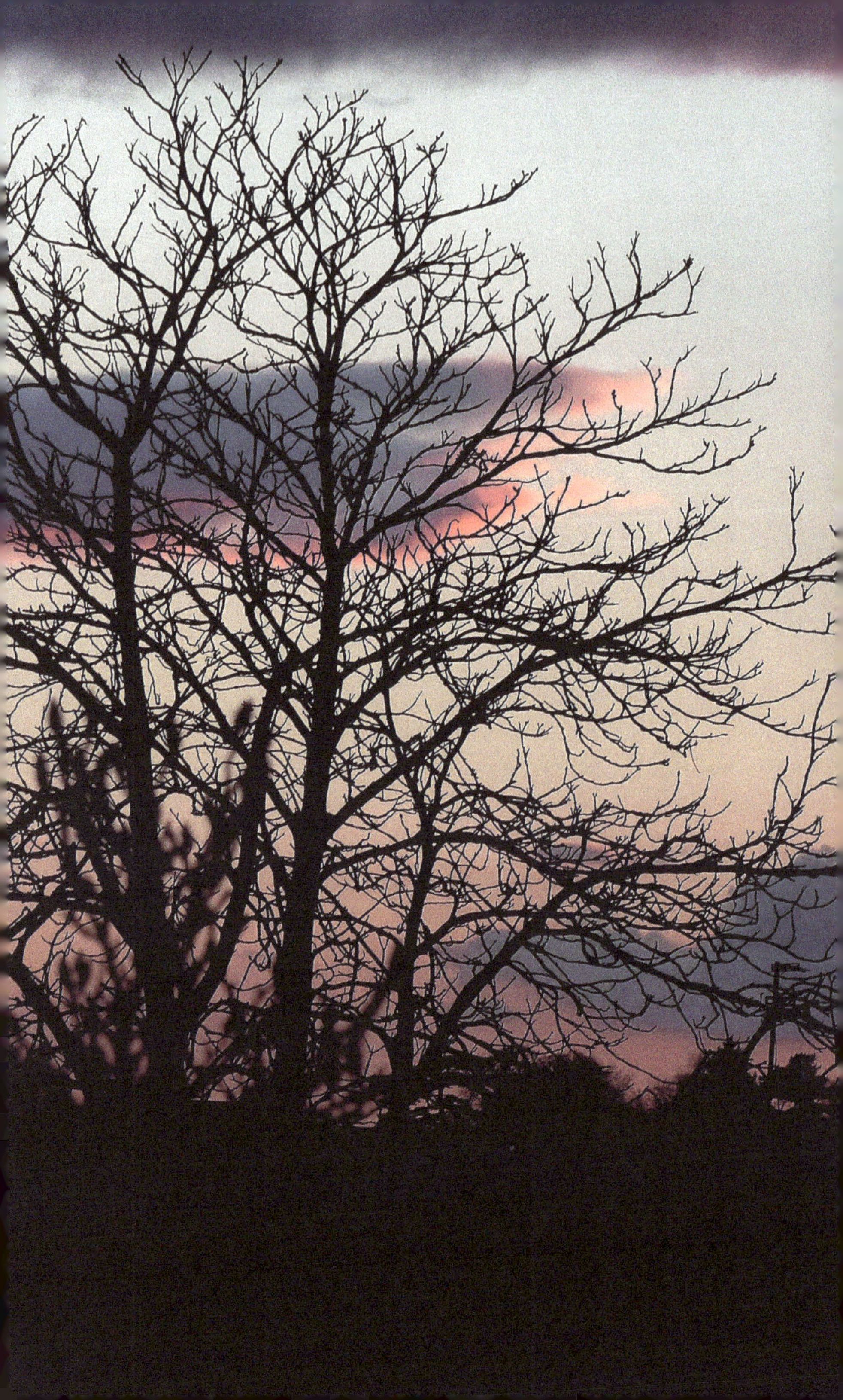

I
MEMORY

Blackberry Picking
In memory of J. Michael Esdaile

Nothing, none of this in Changi prison:
no rag of clothing,
no shard of food,
no hour without pain,
no space less filthy,
no smell less foul,
no shade less burning.

In black-windowed England,
bunks in the cellar,
no night without bombs,
no fruit, no fuel, no paper,
no bread without queues,
no rations without coupons,
always scissors on the counter.

In the shadow of those pasts,
fired and hammered,
lessened, without mass,
we set out by the lake to net
our catch of blackberries.

Others pick only the flawless,
the juicy, the plumply glossy,
the sweet iron-tasty.

We, survivors of Changi,
we, civilian dross from that war,
we spurn nothing:
dusty, seedy, scrawny, wormy,
we snatch them all.

Hedging with Jack

I was fourteen when Jack taught me how to lay a hedge.
I'd left home early, walked over the moors, crossed the
    stream,
climbed the hill. He was waiting by the pile of stakes –
thick leather gloves, billhooks, maul: 'Grab an armful, lad'.

The thorns were unruly, eight feet or more tall.
With the ditch and mound, four feet was enough.
We started at the gate, bent the first stems sharply
down and slashed diagonally across the curve.

The near shoots were trimmed flush to the stub of the gate
    post,
then left longer foot by foot as the distance grew.
We drove stakes in one by one, spaced to hold
the tall wood pressed flat and woven horizontally.

At lunch, Lily picked salad, sliced a fat onion
in vinegar, sweet and sharp with cheese and bread.
We did a long stretch that day, two sides of a field,
a heap of top waste stacked behind us for burning.

Later, farewells, the walk home. I crossed the stream again,
promising next time to raid the stones for trout;
over the moors – rushes, sphagnum, cotton grass,
the land of skylarks and curlews – weary but content.

Love Note to the Rock Under the Bridge

You are the magic mountain with many doors and galleries,
you are the hard green and grey and crystal
sculpted by rain and currents and years endured,
you are the refuge of trout and crayfish and lampreys.

You are the river bedder, the ripple splitter,
the pincer hider, the watersong streamer.

I need you like the splash needs the spray,
I want you like a cliff wants its falling face,
I love you like indigo loves the squeeze of blue
and violet in a waterfall rainbow.

   R – Rilling, trilling, spilling
   O – Overflowing, flood-bestowing
   C – Cascading, overhang-shading
   K – King of skeltering, sheltering

You are the trap where young hands gripped gills,
you are the memory marker where brothers
splashed and laughed and had their fingers nipped,
you are the peakstone above the eddy
where fishermen once cast their mayfly lure.

Take Me Away

Take me away to Thorpe Cloud by the Dove –
the crags, the stepping stones, the lazing trout.
Take me there
in a Morris Traveller
jam-packed with tent, and pots, and you, and love.

I'll wear Dad's green hiking jacket – suits me –
with tweed fly-fisher's fore-and-after cap,
and there you'll be,
sure-booted, goat-footed,
cascading down the steepest sliding scree.

We'll pretend to stumble,
grab hands, enlace,
take off, soar skywards
where the high winds race.

Snake

Bangkok, ca. 1970. The green pit-viper (Trimeresurus macrops) is highly venomous. The pa kao ma *is a comfortable cotton sarong worn at home.*

By the dark front door
fear radiates from the baleful green,
the wood-peg tail,
the yard of folded whiplash.
Phranom slips from the shadows
in sandals and *pa kao ma,*
blade and torch in hand.
The snake tenses, stays coiled,
immobile on the slick marble.
An arm swings, steel bites,
bone and gristle crunch.

The First Dance

Mute protagonist in an absurdist plot,
he lost his life in a random accident.
She blamed herself – how could love not protect? –
and shrank into the dark of the coldest recess.

As winter screwed down, the snow piled,
muffling her numbness. Christmas approached:
she followed the rituals, the warmth,
the music and the chink of glasses.

A quiet hand took hers, led her to the dance.
Decorously, the first three steps,
The first rhythm, the first sway.
Her friends, smiling, hummed along.

A Swim in the Wet

The sky stoops to drench us
as we duck through the wire,
squeeze between the gorse spikes.

We slide across silvered fairways,
ignore the railway's 'Danger' signs,
climb a fence, cross the steel tracks, climb again.

There's a second golf course, stunted brambles,
low sand banks to the beach, gymshoes
just gripping as we hop from rock to rock.

Towels left safe in the waterproof swim bag,
we dash to the sea, wade to our ankles,
to our knees, hold hands in a nesh circle.

'Ring-a-ring-o'-roses,' we yell, 'All fall down!' -
that's how we force the shock, pimpled purple
with cold, water-coloured wet on wet.

Afterwards, sea-salted, between the showers,
we ransack the bag for the elixir
of green ginger wine.

Rock Pools on the Tide Line

Nothing's constant except change, the same old
rhythm of wave and furrow, tide and moon.
Between tides, rock pools transform, starting cold,
warming in the sun, water less salt when

it rains. Caught by the ebb, countless small fry
jink and dart to dodge their subaquatic
hunters. Above, on bared rocks as they dry,
birds swoop on molluscs, marooned, stuck, static –
winkles, whelks and limpets trapped in their shells
air-lifted, dropped and smashed by canny crows,
mussels impaled on oyster-catchers' bills –
while crabs scurry to pick the residues.

The tide swings back, flooding rocks, pools, the small
lethal dramas of predator and prey.
Life ends, life restarts as waves rise and fall,
constant in their careless inconstancy.

An Afternoon Walk in the Jura

Straight up from the track by the church
we skirt the cowsheds on to steep pastures,
a rutted path into the pines and hazels,
the teasel highland ploughed by wild boars' snouts.

On the ridge, a chalet shades the cold spring.
Chain-sawn log benches arc round
a ring of fire-charred stones; inside, cowstalls,
a ladder to the loft, the perfume of hay.

Timbers settle quietly as the sun leaves the valley:
the chalet rests, the day's heat drawing
resins from the cut wood; new night scents
fuse into the rising mountain breeze.

We might not come again before the snow
clamps the high ground. Our hands brush, explore,
capture the shape of our summer faces.
Then, bright in the flattened sun, we head down
the forest track, back to the softer green below.

The wind sends late-day signals as we drop.
A hare, emboldened, halts to stare; deer browse
by the scrub fringe, a fox coughs, owls' wings stir.
We scramble down the hairpins, stride the easy
final stretch, reach home, washed in golden light.

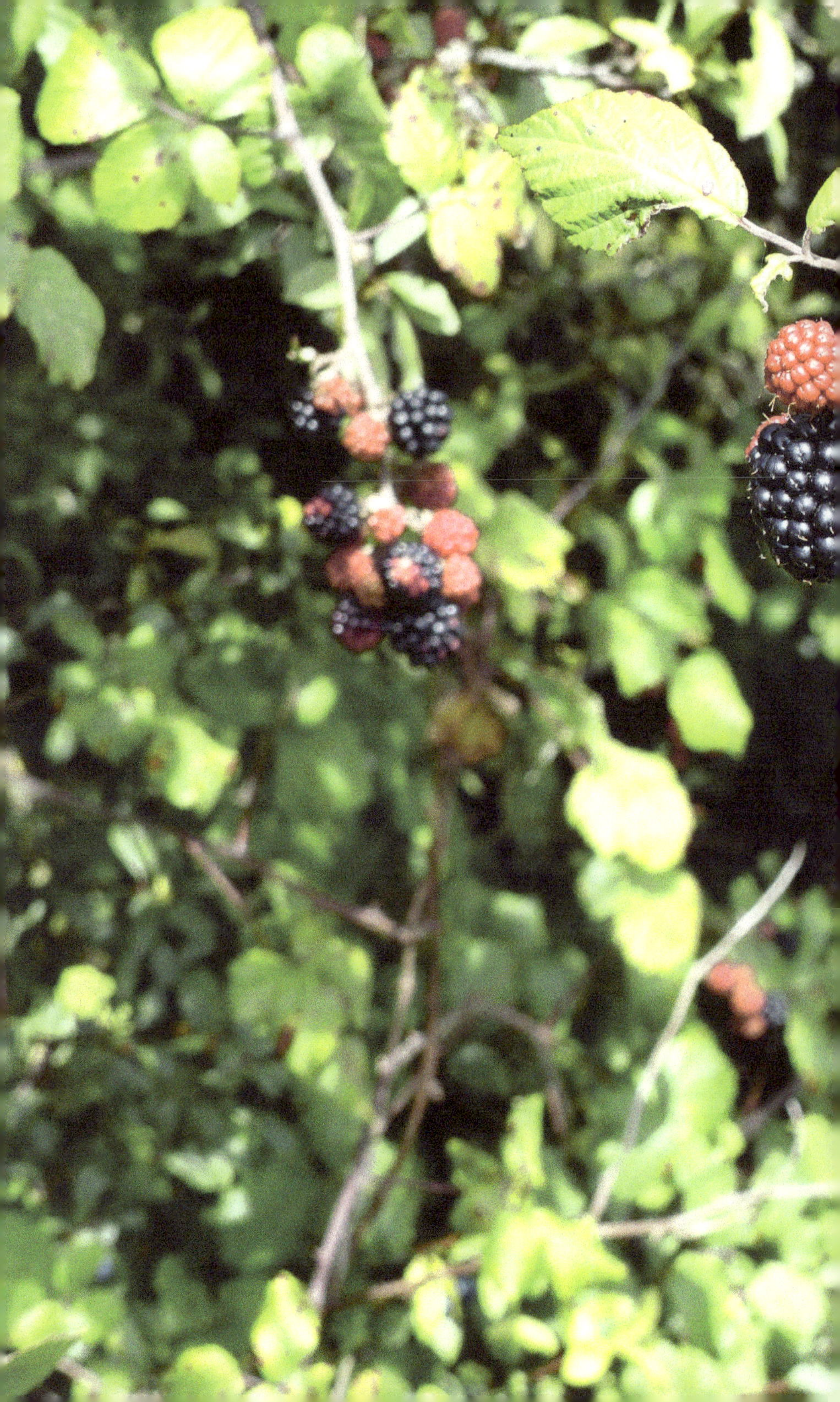

II
LOVING

Prose Poem

You're the poetry and the prose,
the red-hot slam and the prudence of the sage,
the kick of the spoken word
and the patience of the page;
but you dazzle with the rap,
the flash of the flush
and the curl in the toes.

You're the music and the verse,
the during and the after,
the hot stuff in the sun
and the warm rain's laughter;
but yes, crash in with the zap,
the shock of the rush;
there's always time for prose.

You Are My Light
A riff for St Valentine's Day

You are my light
and my delight

the key to wind
my clockwork mind

new melody
that sings to me

the kindling spark
to chase the dark

the melt of frost
with sunstrike burst

your eyes your face
surprised by grace

the longbow tips
of smiling lips

promise of fun
when caring's done

my heart's delight
you are my light

When We Last Met

You told me that I shouldn't, so I didn't;
you told me that I mustn't, so I shan't.

You told me that I hadn't, so I couldn't;
you told me that I wouldn't, so I won't.

You told me that we weren't, so we haven't;
you told me that we daren't, so we aren't.

You told me that we needn't, so we don't.
But life? It wasn't, isn't, doesn't, can't.

Narcissus in Arcadia: A True Romance

It was spring, when magic is never far away,
and the mountain, eerily, promised more than its
    wildness.
A stream spilled down the rock-face
and into a clear basin; insect and bird noises,
the distant piping of a shepherd's flute;
a dipper twitching amid patrolling dragonflies.

I sank on the mossy bank of the pool to rest,
the water mirror-still. My face,
flushed from the climb, stared back.
And then, framed beside me,
I saw the reflection of another face,
nymph-like, mischievous, enchanting.

'Who are you – a dream, a spirit?' I managed to say,
already in thrall to the thousand years of poetry
and music shining from her pearl eyes.
'Who are you?' she repeated, 'Don't you know,
    Narcissus?
They call me Echo. Didn't your father Pan
and your mother Liriope warn you?
You know from them how magic works!'

I splashed the surface of the pool,
and our mirrored images broke
into shards of laughter.
We swam together in the cool water
with the scented forest around us,
and then we lay in the sun to dry.

A Different Silence
Responding to Charlotte Mew's poem 'Arracombe Wood'

Bird-witted? Never:
I too go by the lie of the barley
he sowed, and the smart ranks
of ripened ears of wheat –
all next winter's bread;
his hand on horse and plough,
and his craft with rake and scythe;

the whiskered rye, drilled and risen,
smooth on the bottom acres' swell;
and on the sea of the top field
a sweeping tide of full-grained oats.

Under the yews, his voice, disarticulated,
echoes in a different silence;
no more words spoken to his shadows,
and no mark left in Arracombe Wood.

Living with Dying

There wasn't much to say.
I'd once been sure I'd be the first to go,
and it's a harsh leap from
actuarial guess to diagnosis.
Life shuts down bit by bit:
one week better, one week worse,
maybe flatlining, hoping.

What's left? Farewells, uneasy
loving visits from family and friends,
tracking youngsters' trajectories,
bookmarks in favourite authors,
time with the dogs and cats,
the garden, wild things,
always the sea.

There's no tomorrow: the mind shifts,
looks for any distance closeness allows,
seeks any comfort,
dwells on repeated commonplaces:
we begin to die the moment we're born,
at each age we leave
elements of life behind.

But wait. If you draw existence on a graph,
there's no single line peaking once above the time axis;
each part of the individual has its own line,
its own colour; each quality
will rise or fall through life at its own rate.
As we age, we may run or learn more slowly,
our bodies and desires may change,

yet we live on – as writers write,
painters paint, actors act –
with the same artistry, but a different understanding.

Absence

Autumn: I pick mushrooms under oaks, by myself,
my black dogs my shadows,
wicker basket filling as I circle,
as we used to.

Winter: I feed the birds, by myself,
three dark dogs printing the snow,
cut sprigs of berries for the house,
as we used to.

Spring: I count snowdrops, by myself,
breathe daffodils, say *au revoir* to the small birds
before the leaves fill the trees,
as we used to.

Summer: I tread the beaches, by myself,
walk the dogs, chase the foxes,
paint the flowers, drink cold wine,
as we used to.

At night: I lie, soft-singing to myself
in the bright darkness, your face by mine,
your breath gentle, your body by mine,
as we used to.

If My Heart

If my heart could leave my body,
where would it go, what would it do,
what would it say, what would it feel?

If my heart could leave my body,
it would walk softly across the sand,
plunge with the dogs into sloping water,
dive under quiet waves,
twist like a dolphin to find your heartbeat,
and say, 'It's OK, we're here, we're together,'
and know that this
is where my heart and I will stay.

Totem
For Oscar, prince among Groenendaels

That dark form is not black ivory,
or jet, or basalt;

that shine is not reflected light
from the day's sky;

that sweet waft is not herbs, or hay,
or the drift of late blossom;

that contained strength is not the presence
of a whale, or a shire horse;

that warmth is not the comfort
of a cushion, or a settled cat;

that constancy is not the sureness
of a rock face, or a sense of right.

That is my second self
who walks beside me;

that is my shadow
who guards my dreams.

Love: A Dual Acrostic

Love is an adventure
Often tried –
Value what you build
Each day.

Let your heart
Open, taste the joy;
Vows sustained last for
Ever.

Porcelain Heart

Blessing the clay with Cupid's dart,
Royal Worcester fired a heart,
its whiteness bright, its colours free,
and on the lid a peony.

Useful, too – it's just the thing
for storing all your sweetheart's bling.
And by the flower two butterflies,
flown in to charm her darling eyes.

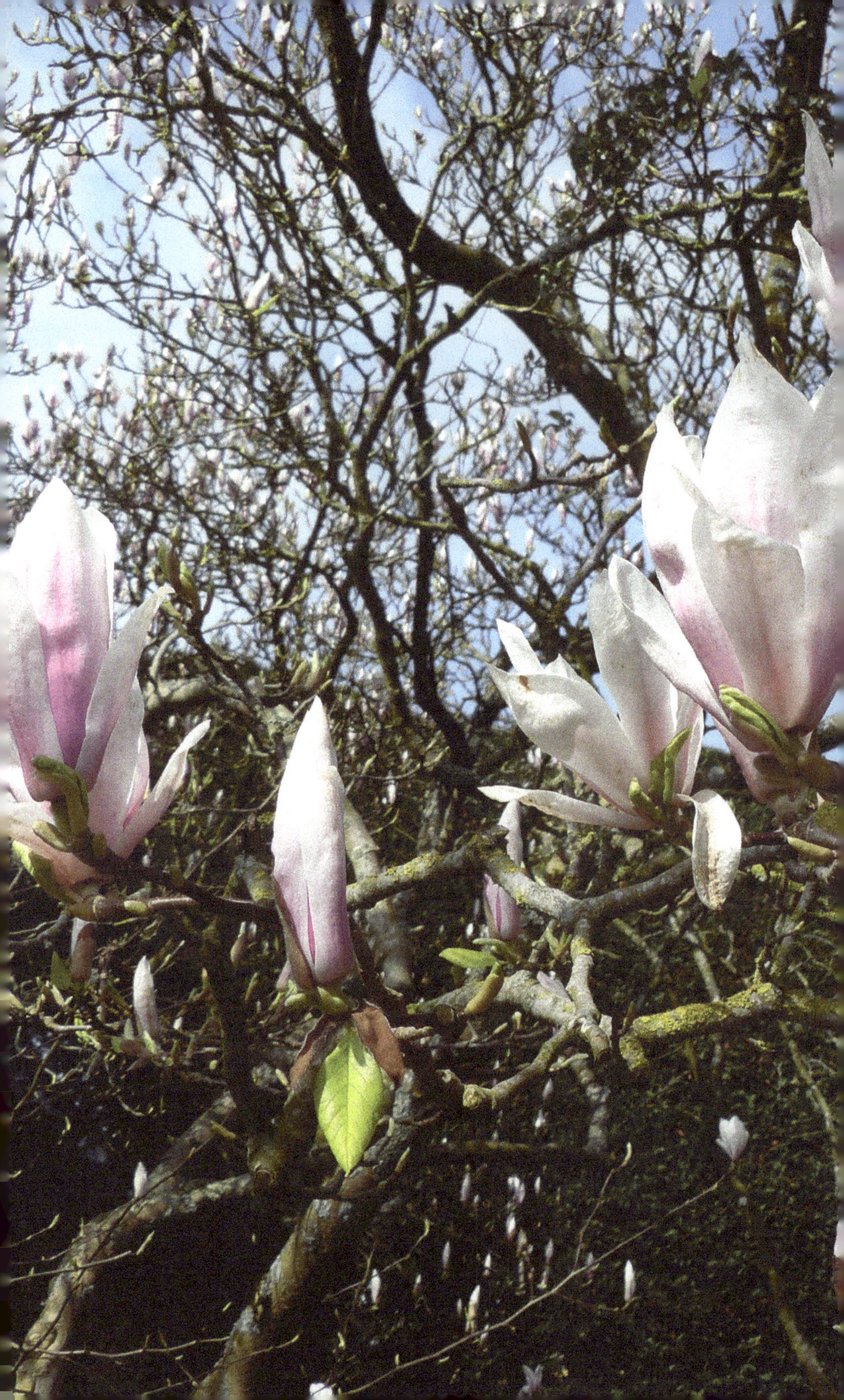

III
THE WAY THINGS ARE

How Was Your Year?

Don't just say lousy. The crows are still there,
they talk in the evenings as they glide
home to the great oak. Sometimes they drop
chicken bones, to read the future.

Not so good for blackberries – been too dry;
they don't last long when the ground's cracked
like a schoolroom map of Africa,
thirst lines ditching abandoned colonies.

There are too many apple trees,
not enough pears. The plums, yes, worth it
for the skin bloom and palette, grading from green
to gold, deepening pink, purple, black.

How was the year? Fair to middling? Not that good?
Must have been some sun, some rainfall?
Yes, but metrics barely noticed, thoughts of nature
    skimped,
in the dirty meteorology of government.

Sorting Pockets

Bits of junk tucked away; safe to assume
the ticket stub's archival, so chuck out;
that ripe, still unsquashed damson's lost its bloom

and wants to be washed and chopped for breakfast.
The cough sweet's wrapping's too brittle now,
too noisy, its just-in-case moment passed.

The handkerchief's fine, handy for my nose
when dust explodes in my sneeze-prone office,
but the paper clip, a flamingo rose,

must join the greens and blues in the oddment
box. In theory I might need the ballast
of coins, useful change to complement

the notes in the back pocket of my jeans;
people still spend money; it still exists,
you need it, I remember what it means.

But I'm going nowhere. The mind resists:
long paper and pen days, writers' routines;
other worlds are distanced; time brakes, persists.

Fruit Salad

It's worth halving shapely blackberries
if you crave that darker taste,
liquid iron on the tongue,
each bisection staining the chopping board
emperor purple.

Strawberries too, sculpted according to size:
wash first, amputate the base,
carve downwards, wedges or quarters.
Or lay sideways, cut off the cone,
slice the rest; taste the red in the raw.

And kiwis – lush emerald in khaki fuzz:
start at the easy end, peel a spiral
of velvet round and round the barrel
to the stub of stalk, hoick out the plug,
cut lengthways or in discs.

Bananas, bonus basics, give two-fold: first
the skin, split into ribands, a bundle of
strops chopped in inch-lengths of instant compost,
and then the white torpedo inside,
dice and roundels, cubes and rings.

The best paring knife? Must be honed
and handily balanced - not too short or long,
not too thick or thin. Forget that Roman tale
about the longer sword that beat the Picts;
it wasn't much use for chopping fruit and veg.

Enough

Way past 'Best before',
too stale for any taste-bud future,
fancy lime and ginger notwithstanding,
the salad dressing teeters,
musters its chilled courage,
takes quick leave of the milk and butter,
dives from its ledge,
slams the tiles,
rolls away dismembered,
the wet crunch of shards glistening
in an ochre hexagon of oil.

They do this, glass artefacts;
they call time on life, opt for
an exit by dustpan and brush.
Cups and plates do it too,
choosing the slippery finality
of a soapy sunset,
the fracas of chip and crack.
It's more than Weltschmerz,
more like plain 'Enough'.
Time for the leap from the fridge,
the crash by the sink:
the pigeon's surrender to the hawk.

Languages Like These

My row of grammars and fat dictionaries
doesn't help me much to understand
why I love so many languages – it's more
the places and people, what we ate and drank,
the sights and sounds, the smells, the land.

I love Welsh for the mountains, the choirs,
Moel Hebog and Beddgelert, slate hillsides, Anglesey's
beaches; Breton for pancakes and Quimper bagpipes;
Norwegian for trolls, Hardanger fiddles in wooden
    churches,
the port in Bergen, breakfast goat cheese.

Italian, of course: vaporetti in Venice,
northern lakes, ice-cream and Verdi in Rome,
Etruscan tombs, the stifled south;
and French for the Gascon wines and sunflowers
of the Gers, the quays of Paris, once my home.

And Spanish – Ibiza's old town, the Prado,
a cueca in Santiago, a pasodoble in Mexico.
Then German – the Bernese Oberland, Vienna Woods,
fruit tart with whipped cream in the Zillertal,
Heidelberg's castle, Neuschwanstein under snow.

But what of Russian, anchored deep in roughshod dreams?
Brutal, tearful, the key to Slavic mystery –
steppe, sleigh bells, Stenka Razin, vodka, Moscow nights.
Should I still love it? Maybe, if Turgenev and Tchaikovsky
can outweigh the Kremlin's power-stained history.

Retrograding
A pantoum

To have an empty day ahead
Back to the telephone at last
In the dark, relaxed in bed
I thought those simple days were past

Back to the telephone at last
Pick up and answer, scowl or smile
I thought those simple days were past
When all you had to do was dial

Pick up and answer, scowl or smile
Forget the colour of your shirt
When all you have to do is dial
It's fun to let go, to revert

Forget the colour of your shirt
Forget the way the menfolk shave
It's fun to let go, to revert
Remember how to misbehave

Forget the way the menfolk shave
If any do – the bear look's in
Remember how to misbehave
Relish tasting trivial sin

If any do – the bear look's in
If you prefer, stay in the dark
Relish tasting trivial sin
Whisper nothings, sweet night talk

If you prefer, stay in the dark
That's how the world goes off to bed
Whisper nothings, sweet night talk
Another empty day ahead

Resculpting

Blocks of marble, chunks of wood
don't volunteer; maybe,
if you're lucky, they acquiesce.
You don't hear three tons of Carrara
pleading 'Maestro, bring your genius,
inside this mass is a masterpiece
waiting to be released'.
Or a blank slab of ripe oak
begging for revelation:
'Wield your artist's chisel,
carve me like butter,
use me like clay'.

But here I am, volunteering,
climbing on to the trestle,
easing into the cushions,
accepting the blue overshoes,
choosing music on a whim.

Numbed by a score of needles, I submit.
'Surgeon, carve the flesh, find that clear core:
more needle, more knife, a new blade;
burn and stitch – shape the form
buried within this imperfection'.

Later, at home in the garden,
I smell the clemency of purple roses,
feel the breeze on the cut face I can't see,
clumsily sip half a beer.

I'm dodging the mirror, but

there must be a name for it,
the syndrome where the imprisoned figure
learns to love its sculptor.

Retreat from the Edge

The self – mind and body –
that used to fly as one in dreams
now splits. The mind flies alone,

rises, circles, looks down
from the edge, almost ready,
almost free, on the emptied form.

But its shadow re-lives
a life of near-deaths:
fevers, a drowning boy,
a car skidding on its roof,

frontiers crossed under the tanks' guns,
Andean skyfalls, missed runways,
a yacht's broken rudder,
a collapsing mountain path.

It's still too soon. Captive to memory,
the mind won't relinquish its dramas.
It slips back into the body,
free enough for now.

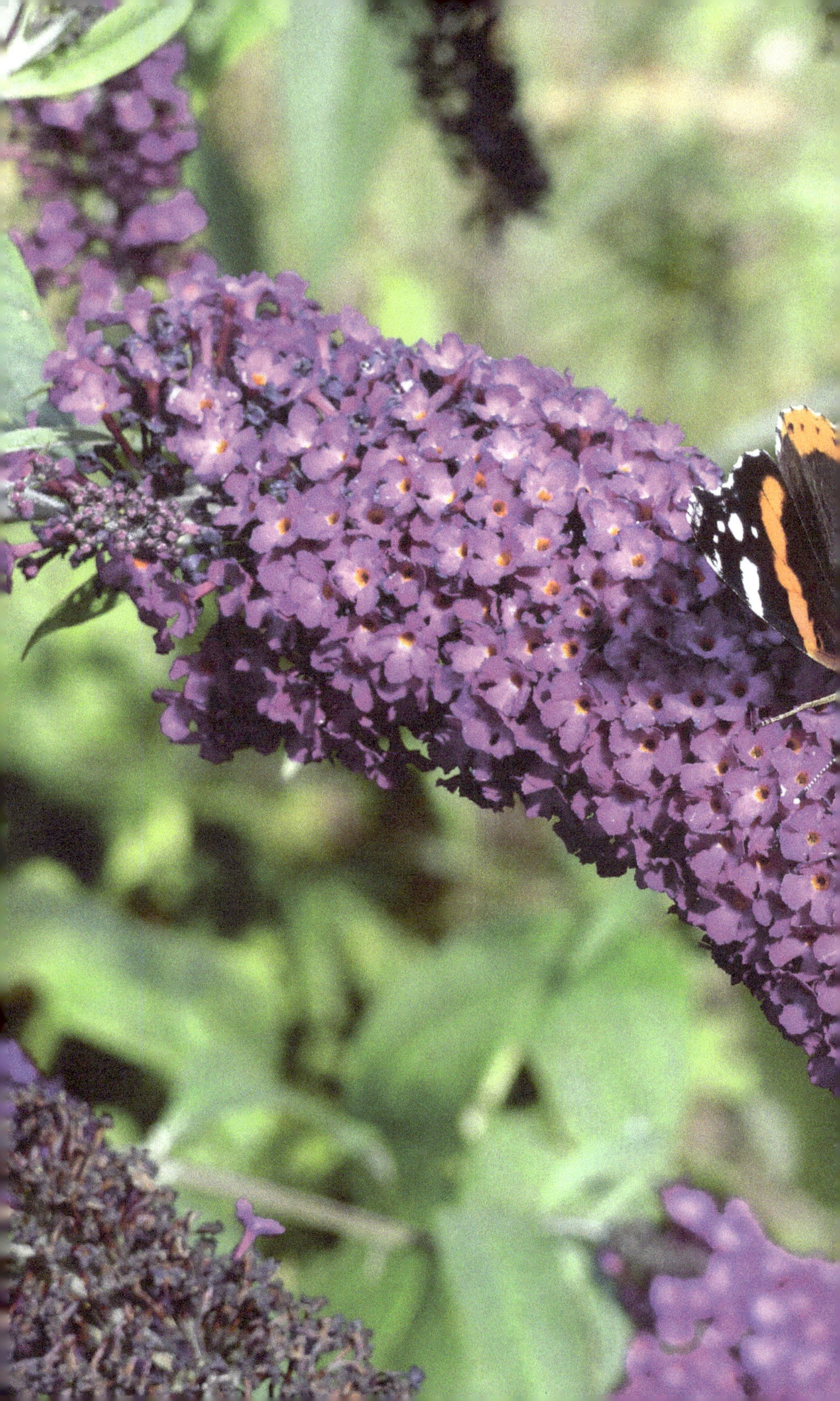

IV
ECOSYSTEMS

Winning the Race to Zero

It's hotting up: chaos warps the Arctic silence
as ice cracks and shovels dig permafrost for fossil pipelines;
polar bears raft south, swept on a tide of plastic icebergs;
bird migrations pause – the north is warm and green enough,
southern wetland nest sites no longer safe from predators.

At the other, Antarctic pole of desecrated Earth
penguins and seals are unwilding, re-skilling;
they're learning to sweat, untie strangleholds of castaway
fishing nets, cough up microplastics, make suncream
from fishbones and bladderwrack boiled in new-bared rock
    pools.

Between the poles, felled and burning forests, wastelands
of exhausted soil, silent poisoned springs. Is there a better way?
Imagine hope's weather vane, aiming its arrowed neck
at a different future: crashing carbon counts, fading fossil fuels,
new energies that point a path to life ahead.

You know the science: air, fire, water, earth, each element
abused, exploited, polluted, made unfit for life.
And as the water rises, will we float our dinghies, build on stilts,
cram people, animals, vaccine labs and food banks
on the sparse archipelagos of island hilltops?

Evolution? Sure, we can endure, speed-learn survival,
but we don't have the eons that moths took to mimic twigs or
    roll out
nectaring tongues, that zebras needed to paint the stripes
that break their silhouettes, that giraffes spent to reach
and graze the tallest tree, watchful for fire and kill.

So action now! Don't just talk the COP talk; rewards must be earned. Can we stabilise greenhouse gases, can we 'prevent anthropogenic interference with the climate system'? Can we beat the doom of time, adapt ecosystems, make the desert bloom?
Surely, eight billion of us! Let's sustain life, join hands, win the race to zero.

Running Out Of Time

In autumn 2022 the Running Out Of Time relay run carried a message from the young people of Glasgow (site of COP26) and points along the way to world leaders gathered for COP27 in Sharm el-Sheikh, some 7700 km to the south.

It's a long hard dusty road from Glasgow
to Sharm el-Sheikh, a trail spanning eighteen flags,
a chain of stages, countless pounding strides,
to drive home the climate crisis message:
we're running out of time.

So let us run together, work to convince,
engage belief and stoke the media fire;
along the way, ignite the energy
of a thousand schools, draw hope from science
and the spark of new solutions.

The relay baton's a smart messenger,
a high-tech capsule, more than a symbol –
an icon of urgency, from human
hand to hand, country to country.

Its message, from tomorrow's leaders to today's:
act together, use your power, reset
priorities, think future, reach higher,
keep Earth alive. The target's vast, and yet
it's nothing, net zero, now or never.
Quick, we're running out of time.

Together

We're different, but equal: let's start there.
The weight of our joy and pain
isn't defined by rank or beauty;
the value of what we feel
doesn't depend on an educated brain.

However clever our words, our perceptions,
that's not the measure of our voice.
Our thoughts may have no special virtue:
what counts is their human, complicit sum –
they'll never be the perfect church choir's choice.

We're flawed, so don't insist on righteousness,
or constant sense, or armies of reason,
or navies of facts, or peer-group
pressured correctness; you may find
our music off-beat, off-key, out of season.

Yet with the threads of our diversity
we'll weave a force for all, not just the few.
Together we can mend the Earth's fragile
safety net, build a fair society:
is that too much – to save the world, save you?

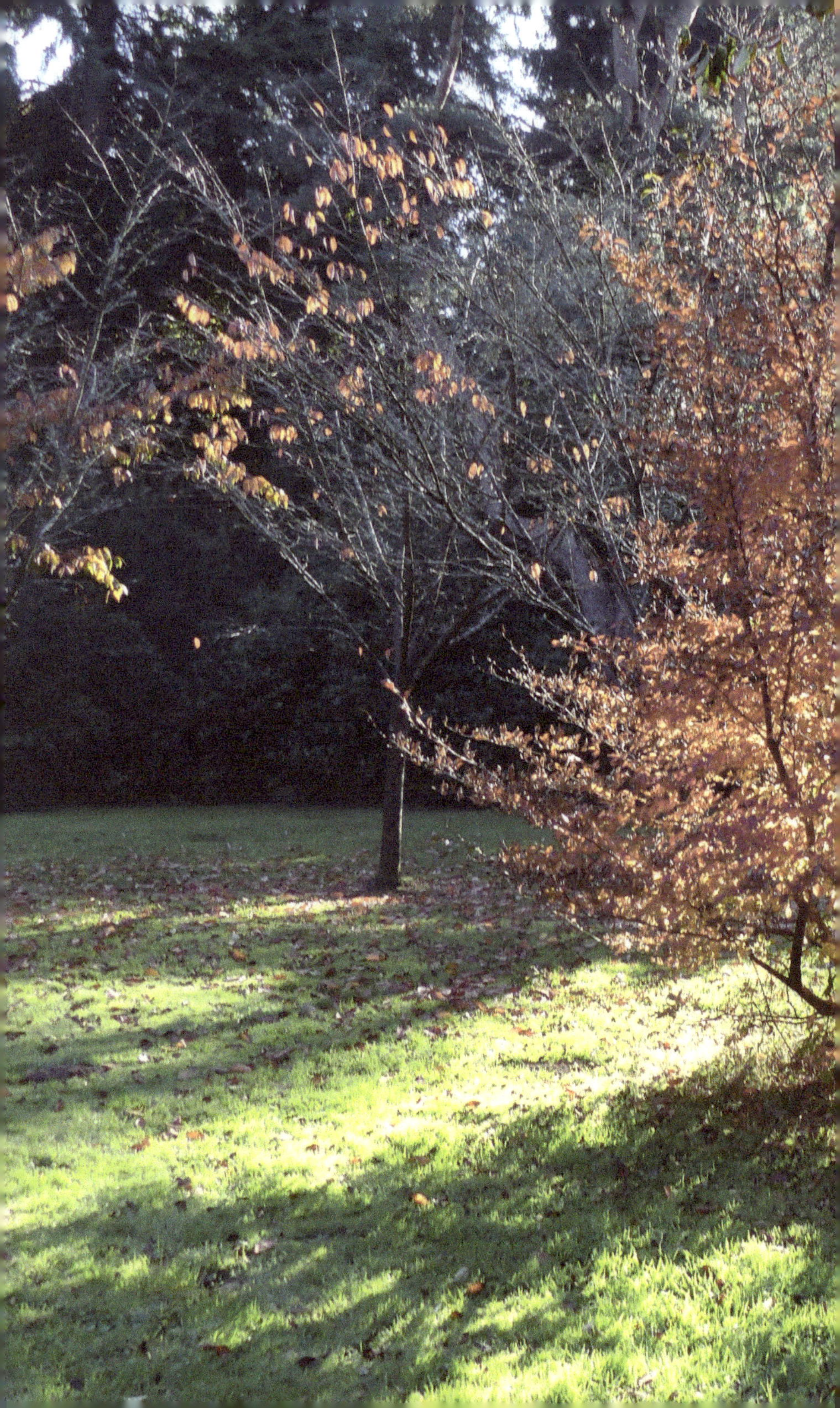

V
GARDENS

February Storm

Did I imagine, through the smothered glass,
the cyclic whirl of butterflies?
Were the backlit shadow dancers
no more than leaves spinning kites in the storm?

Those bolts from the edge of vision,
shot between the strata of the sky,
were they the flash of arrowing birds,
contesting - deriding - the gale's boasting?

Was it right, frustrating the plundering snails,
to rescue the garden's single golden blossom,
a daffodil in fat bud flattened by the wind,
to drink indoors its wry-scented glow?

Modest Winter
In tribute to Frome Wildlife Watch

It's quiet in the nature reserve.
Seems no-one's home, but hold your nerve.
You can't ever know who'll be there;
you'll see the species you deserve

Me, I'd love to spot an otter,
or perhaps a beaver – what a
treat! – or hairstreak, or spoonbill pair
if the earth keeps getting hotter.

But all I ever find is slugs –
the really common kind – and bugs.
I never see, high in the air,
a harrier as it swings and shrugs.

However hard I'm wildlife hunting
I never see a stoat or bunting,
or polecat, kingfisher or hare,
hear lizards skid or wild boar grunting.

Though fish are jumping splashy rings,
the swans stay sulking in the wings.
Those fancy ducks have gone elsewhere,
dabbling in unimagined things.

Yet reed-beds hiding birds away,
and iffy pawprints in the clay,
and dead seed-heads, twigs winter-bare,
are ample for this winter's day.

Forgiving the Judas Tree

In spring bees clamour when the petals burst
from their swollen winter sepal capsules,
tingeing from red to darkish pink, spacing
each flower on lengthening pedicels.

The blossoms cluster pea-shaped, sweet-nectared,
each flower complete – banner, fused keel, wings,
pollen-loaded stamen. The filament,
soon fertilised, becomes the dangling pod.

Then the zigzag of alternating leaves,
first bronzed, red-edged, then green, lighter on the
reverse, palmate, rounded, almost heart-shaped,
yellowing in autumn before the fall.

Green pods hang like roosts of bats from the trunk
and branches, near-translucent when the light's
behind them, seed nodes X-rayed by the sun,
turning dark brown brittle as they ripen.

I see the buds' beauty, not beads of blood;
the pods' harvest, not hanging mannekins.
But even if the Judas myth were true,
I'd want forgiveness to heal the false kiss.

Painting the Ginkgo

Tradition says ginkgos are for healing.
Never doubting, I head for the park;
I need to see my old migrant
friend, breathe its bark, twin-lobed leaves,
rank fruits, fossil strangeness.
Matt green in summer,
gold in autumn.
I'm ready
now to
paint.
Start with
soft pencil
on stiff paper,
unscrew water jar,
grip the palette, squeeze out
bright tints, choose a likely brush.
No need for macerated seeds
or therapeutic leaves: I drink the
ginkgo's poised stillness, and we're both made whole.

Sightlines

The hare's head on a conifer tip;
three spikes of yellow flag, precursors
of the bannered insurrection by the pond;
an upstart quince between two apples;
a cobnut crouching beneath the parapet
of a reef of roses;

laburnum walled behind the willow;
tall seedheads of fritillaries camouflaged
like skinny giraffes in the savannah of unmown grass;
wild roses festooning the mix of shrubs;
pyracantha blossom, lighthouse white
after the wash of rain.

And rounding blind corners,
bent spokes arcing from the eye's hub,
sightlines curve to find those names, that beauty –
weigela, buddleia, crassula, betula,
peonies, cranesbill, giant scarlet poppies.
Seen or unseen, the flowers exist;
that was the sense of creation.

Time Out of War

Must be weekend: the crows
glide in, beaks freighting
cast-off barbecue buns;
they find the birdbath has its uses –
dunk, swizzle, slurp, gobble.

They don't wait for me to leave:
the game's more relaxed while
the referee's still there, on the bench,
eyes watchful, hand busy
with pen and paper,
or stretching to pick cashews
from a carved Manila bowl, or
refuelling with amber ale.

The garden birds tell me I'm a talisman
against killer cats and kestrels.
The lawn comes alive, not just the crows:
blackbirds hop, scanning the grass,
pigeons waddle poolside,
a robin's song caps the dead prunus.

Just time for a swig from the pond;
the truce is short and sweet
before evening dies.

Mousetrap

The crows were rowdy this afternoon,
the way they are when they brainstorm,
barely hidden in the last thinned spearheads
of the willow's skyline.

Later, on the mosaic of bronze leaves
beneath, patterned too early by the drought,
I found a mousetrap, one kill from new,
bait and catch vanished.

I supposed the crows, scouting gardens,
had found a loaded trap, flown it to the tree top,
prised the victim free from the spring,
and let it fall, wood and wire.

Under the moon, I cut a sheaf of lavender,
incense to mourn small creatures.
Crows, don't wait: there won't be a re-set.
I have no use for mousetraps.

Red Admiral

Ten apples – red, green, gold –
in two ranks on the old
terrace table, call to
fieldfares, winter totems
moving south from the cold.

As magnolia leaves fall,
branches lighten, rise; tall
heads no longer stoop, but
duck for the thorn berries'
arching weight by the wall.

A red admiral, late
basking, adjusts the tilt
of its broad solar wings,
glides a circuit, resists
the pull to hibernate.

Autumn Wind-Down

Empty wisps of blackberries
mark the change, fallen apples
waiting grass-cupped for the slugs.

The willow's thinned, scalp bared;
pigeons partner dark crows,
blue-tits flit to scant twigs.

Dead-heading's spurred banks
of late-bloom roses,
sharp in the crisp dawn.

Scarlet hips and
yellow berries
stud the hedges.

October:
feel autumn,
plan winter.

Warmth, a
roof, food
in store.

Eyes
closed;
sleep.

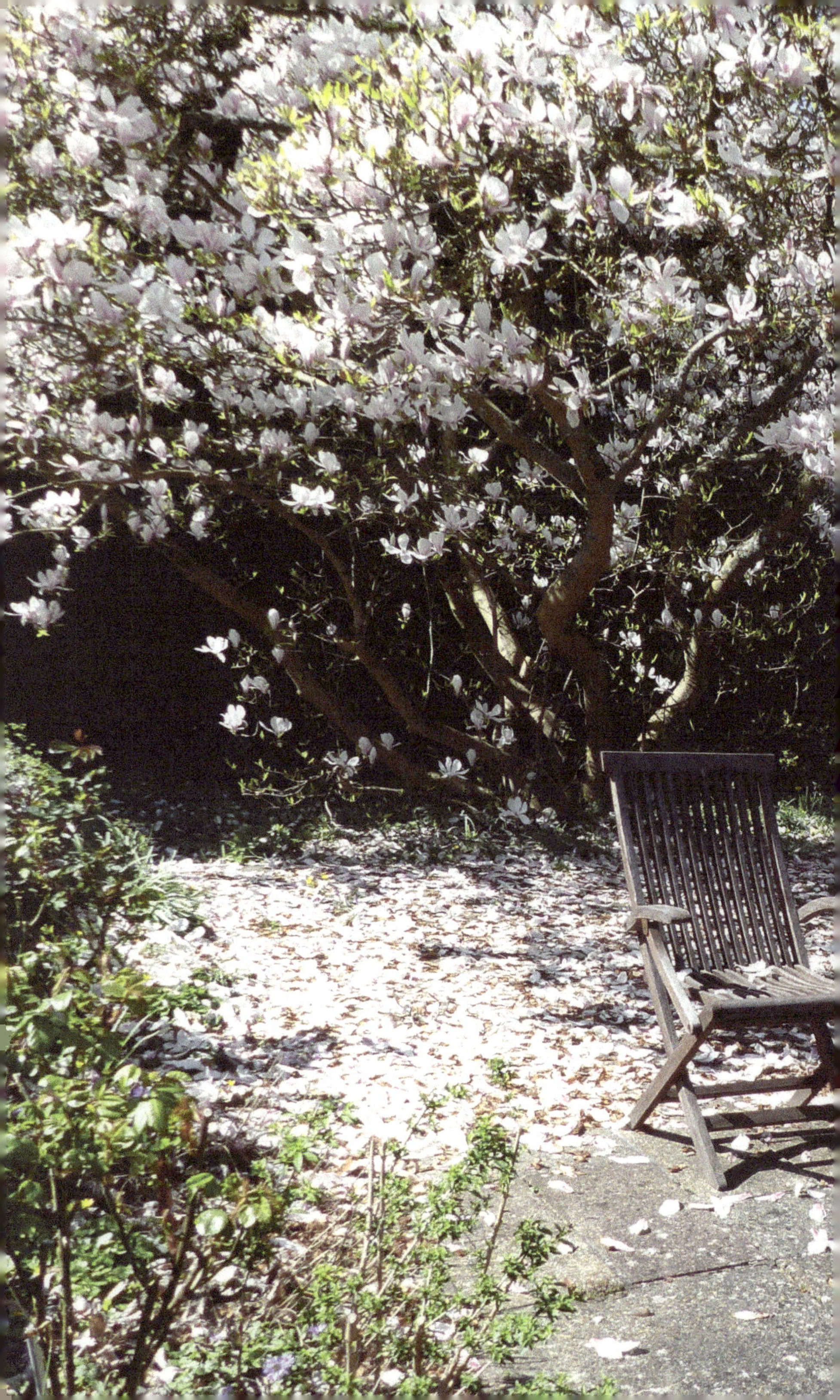

VI
GALLERY VOICES

Pinhole
*'Slow Time', Somerset Art Works' exhibition of
   solargraphics, Black Swan Arts, Frome, 15 January-27
   February 2022*

Wired to lockdown, my can-camera hung calcified
in the stillness of a thousand indecisive moments.
In my childhood bedroom, I remember
instant images on the wall, projected
through the chink in the early morning curtains.
Time-lapse, strangled in shadow, hasn't worked like
    that:
more like a face worn into patient paper,
layered from ancient light,
some of it reaching earth, some skipping
or pausing time, sinking into the tomb
of the camera's fourth dimension,
processed by the computer, by our perception.

I'm unsure of this visual language:
I see flares and cut-outs in guarded darkness,
X-rayed ribs of architecture,
the gradual structure of a tree,
and translate each shade into conflicts of meaning –
too slow, too fast, too trivial, too huge –
as ivy grows to block the pinhole in the can.

Iterations
A tour of Linda Burgess's exhibition 'On Repetition', Black Swan Arts, Frome, 4 June-3 July 2022

Eighty-five stubby, shiny-capped sawn-off pipes,
a mute marimba, three notes short of a full piano;
a mighty folded red-on-red-on-red seaside sunset;
five shallow aluminium frames, laying down laws

in coded strips of black-squared moon language;
twice times nine polished bars ridging rusty metal,
one raft proud on the wall, the other foot-wipe flat;
a low-pitched Chinese factory, the fifteen slabs

of its auspicious red roof ripe for solar panels;
an upright oblong, patterned under plastic
with obsessive 1970s repetition,
embroidered to the left with lacy light and shadow;

three giant curls from a Breton-flag butter block,
white-and-black – or are they black-and-white?
And two flayed dinosaur skins, trimmed and waxed,
one dark, one lighter burgundy, half 2D levels,

half 3D foothills, in grained metal trays.
A room of craft, discipline, adherence to the Rule:
everything's repeated, nothing's the same;
each iteration co-exists, is co-material, in repeated time.

A Duet of Lines
Mini-pantoum responding to pen and ink drawings by Guy Watts and Daniel McGirr, Black Swan Arts, Frome, 5 March-3 April 2022

The art of life's a skein of wool, a bowl of pasta,
scowling from its black-barred geometry.
Across the room, the infinite exactitude
of a perfect universe inked on a pin's head.

Scowling from its black-barred geometry:
imagine the cities, trees, gardens of the moon's ley lines,
of a perfect universe inked on a pin's head –
could they bud-burst in a spring of binary colour?

Imagine the cities, trees, gardens of the moon's ley lines
across the room, the infinite exactitude.
Could they bud-burst in a spring of binary colour?
The art of life's a skein of wool, a bowl of pasta.

Stump in Wartime
Alex Faulkner's 'The Uprooted Stump of Seahenge Rising in Front of the Nachi Falls' (gesso on paper), Artists for Ukraine exhibition, Black Swan Arts, Frome, 1-24 April 2022

Maybe it's not an intubated,
dismembered Baconian torso;
nothing anatomical,
not limbless Grecian marble,
no head blown off, no missing hands,
no legs gone walk-about.

It's more like a vessel of clouded glass,
the stumpy shape of a see-through shirt
hanging white on blue like stiff Delft laundry,
uprooted, inverted, caught between movement.
And behind, the patterned boards, windowless
towers as yet unbombed, not yet falling,
ridged with the skyward grain
of the cratered wheatfields over the fence.

The shape becomes a chalice, empty, waiting:
waiting for sunflowers, for peace,
for the sun to break cover,
waiting for its white to brim with yellow
against the blue flag of the sky.

The Life of Rocks
Simon Hitchens' exhibition 'Beyond Body', Black Swan Arts, Frome, 30 April–26 May 2022

We feel that rocks live, and embody life,
but is that a mere projection of our want?
Or is it we who exist only because
the rocks see or imagine us?

Are these representations, these forms,
the after-lives of the post-human world,
vitrified in the ultra-kiln of atomic nemesis,
or are they prototypes, maimed glimpses of
the still incandescent pre-life
before the protozoan soup, long before humans,
before we roomed in rocks, carved stone tools,
painted cave walls with the souls of animals?

Mostly, we're explorers; we verify
the rock's sentience through the life in its veins.
We follow water as it teases through the fissures,
we trace the glint of seams of gold,
and then we pipe and crack and delve and dynamite.
That's no relationship; but still the rocks endure.

Shortcut to Provence
*Black Swan Arts Open, Frome, Summer 2022: Rosey
    Prince's oil on canvas 'Shortcut' and Wendy Lovegrove's
    charcoal 'Hilltop Village, Provence'*

There's a universe of form, a clamour
of images: people, animals and plants,
abstracts, embedded words, smart tech,
noisy colour, quieter shade.
You wonder, would you have chosen these,
could you have created that?
Did the crowding of visions make you
want to smell the paint, grab a brush,
finger the paper, choose the frame?
Would you have dreamt
an embroidered dog held in tattooed arms?

I narrow the mood, go binary
to the gallery's black-and-white section,
open blankly to silhouettes,
tiny obsessive lines, shadings and splodges,
shamans dancing in the heads of beasts
round a henge I feel I once knew.

I end in an obscure corner, by an oil
of background buildings half-screened by foliage.
I duck under the dark trees, taking the shortcut
round the corner to summer holidays in Provence.
I'm in the charcoal soul of my hilltop village,
drunk on the purple scent of lavender.

Girl with the Square Helmet
Cath Bloomfield's exhibition 'A Vocabulary of Making Revealed,' Black Swan Arts, Frome, 17 September- 23 October 2022

I. Upside
'Under my helmet,' she said, 'sits my iron-cube brain,
armour ribbed to catch your sword.'

> 'But why the peek-a-boo breasts,
> why the gulch of unprotected belly?'

'To draw your eyes, to lure your thrust,
to make us equal, giver and giving.'

> 'And you don't mind the clink of visors
> as my caged lips feel for yours?'

'I know my trammelled head,
my hammered heart, my accoutred eyes,
will escape their metal frame,
find and taste your pith.'

> 'And I'll glue us, weld our spirits
> belly to belly, nipple to nipple -
> there'll be no gap in the collage
> between our ochre skins.'

II. Downside
'Lost one,' I said, 'how fettered is your heart?
Are all its circles square ?
I see your breasts pinched flat, the shadowed part,
but not the sun's share.'

'I'm encased in rough-forged metal,
refracting emptiness,
a sterile bouquet with no petal,
void of happiness.'

'We've got it wrong, and I'm hard shade;
my squared brain too is frozen,
when once my universe was made
of layers of life well chosen.'

'And in the past we danced, joy was defended,
I didn't need my scrapheap armour;
but then I just pretended
to smile above grief's clangour.'

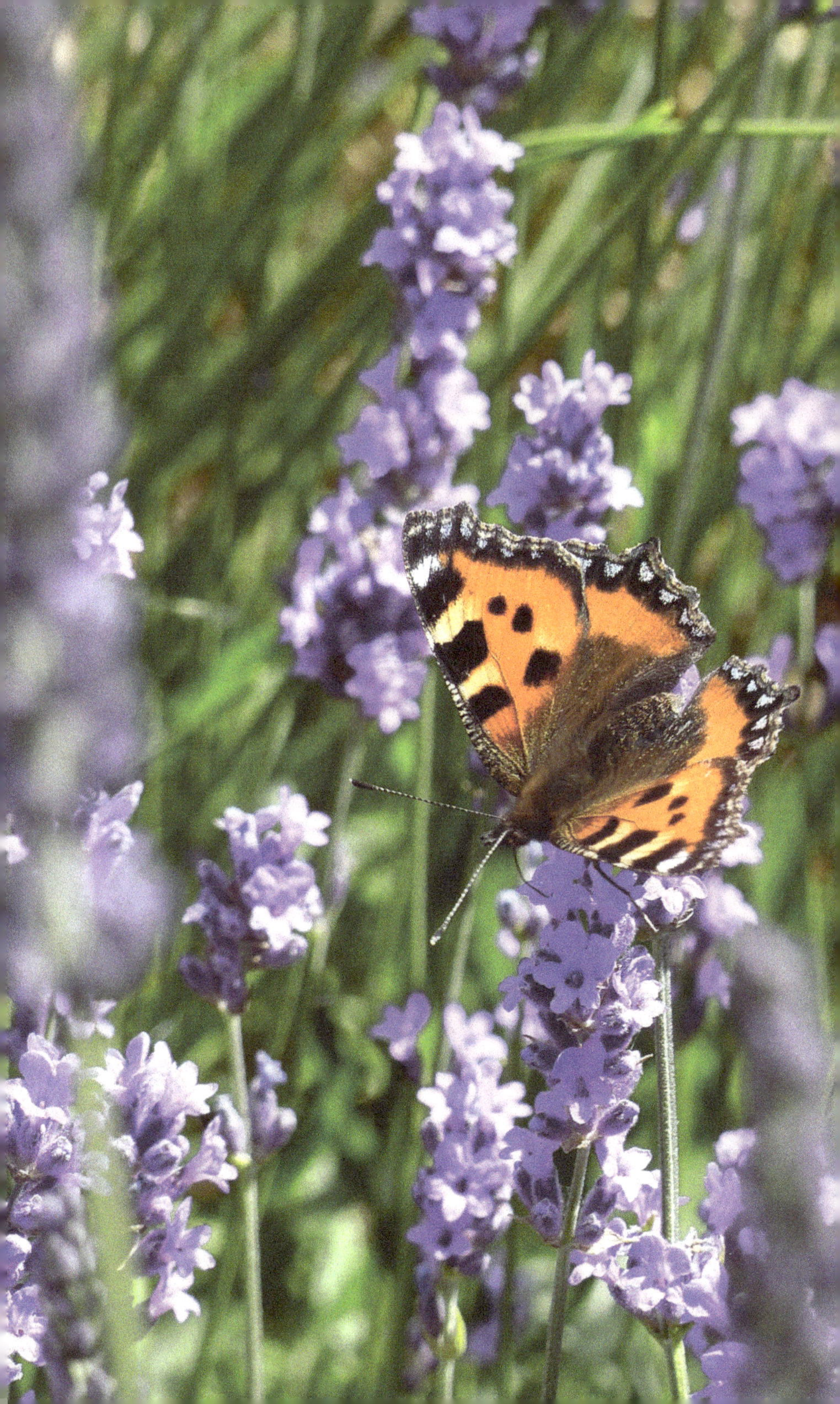

VII
ENCOUNTERS

Promise the Earth

'It's all yours,' said Adam.
'Thanks, love,' said Eve,
'I do like a nice garden.'
'Just one thing,' said Adam.
'Yes?' said Eve.
'That damned serpent,' said Adam.
'Yes?' said Eve.
'Sometimes it spoils things.'
'It'll be OK,' said Eve.
'Would you like an apple?'

Minor Operation

The phone rings. I jump – first call this week.
Seasoned admin voice; they've had a cancellation.
'Can you come to the city hospital next Monday?'
How to get there? No, that won't work.
Last summer they promised it'd be
on the doorstep, here in town.
'Very kind, thanks for the thought,
but I'd rather wait; then I can walk from home.'
After ten months, I'd almost managed to forget.
'OK, we'll hang on for a slot there;
and you can be sure, you're on the list,
you're not forgotten.'

Taxi

Not too good, mate.
Had Covid a fortnight ago, bloody
slew me. Then the flu straight after,
but couldn't take time off –
other guys were away, isolating.

Couple of days ago, did my back in –
went and lifted something too heavy by half.
My dad's seventy-six and still working;
wanted to show him I can do it too –
you forget you aren't as young as you were.

Today the mobile holder broke – what else
can go wrong? Won't say, in case it happens;
you never know what's round the corner.
See this cushion? Really helps; it's got
three tabby kittens sown on it – feel the warmth.

Climbing the Kerb

Nice day! Don't meet
many people on the street.
Not much fun being old, is it?
Not so easy to get around.
Some say it's better than the alternative –
not always so sure.

How do you get on with your stick?
Big help? Extra leg?
I always say it's just a prop,
only for show, to fight off the fans.
Expect you saw me climb the kerb –
do all my own choreography.

I'm off to the post box now;
it's a couple of hours before collection time,
should make it.
Sending off my last cheque –
don't know what I'll do then.
My bank's so secure,
can't get into my account.
Yes, I'm on internet, sort of,
but mostly I'm pretty antisocial;
just do – weird name – 'social media'.

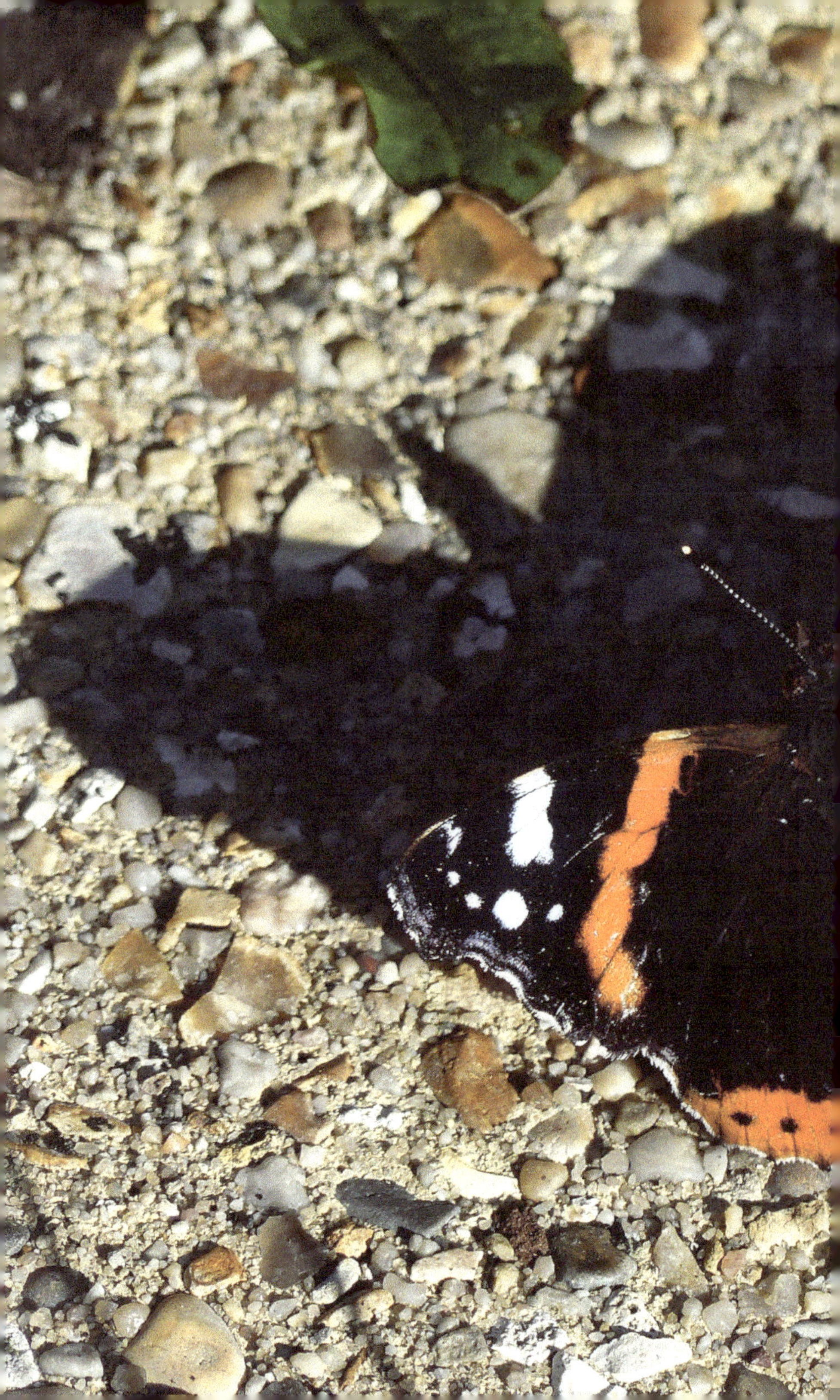

VIII
SONGS AND STORIES

Sharing: The Animals' Welcome Carol
Dedicated to the Frome Youth Choir. First performed, to the author's melody, at the Choir's Christmas concert, 7 December 2019

Joseph, will you share our roof?
The inn's packed out, it's nearly dawn.
Our starlit stable's quiet and safe
For Mary's baby to be born.

Angels told us you would come,
The shepherds brought you simple food.
While Mary nurses her young son,
Will you share our figs and bread?

There's water in these wooden pails,
Enough to cool you, rinse the dust.
Sweet Mary, will you share with us
To bathe the babe and quench your thirst?

Jesus, Lord, will you share our hay,
A manger full, so soft and deep?
Doves will sing a lullaby;
While angels watch, we'll guard your sleep.

Chorus
The ox and the ass,
The sheep and the dove,
We'll share all we have –
Our warmth and our love.

Happy New Year!
In tribute to Clement Moore's 'The Night Before Christmas'

'Twas the week after Christmas, when all through the house
Not a creature was idle, not even a mouse.
Each hole in the stockings was mended with care
In the hope that St Nick would revisit next year.
The children were playing – they'd tidied their beds –
With flavours of mandarins fresh in their heads,
While mamma in her apron and I in chef's hat
Were teasing our brains with cookery chat,
When out on the lawn there arose such a chatter,
I rushed from the stove to see what was the matter.
The sun on the flank of the frost-laden grass
Cast ornithological shadows en masse:
Four crows, two magpies, a pepper of sparrows,
Three pigeons, a blackbird, and where the lawn narrows,
A goldfinch, a robin so lively and quick
I thought how their movements would charm old St Nick.
More rapid than reindeer my feathered friends came,
And I clicked with my tongue and called them by name:
"Now, *Croaker*! now *Goldie*! now *CheepCheep* and *Squawk*,
Come feast on the fatballs and swap birdseed talk."
With beaks full of sunflower and twitching tails merry,
They hopped through the roses and perched on the cherry.
Up to the treetops the songsters they flew,
With the spirit of Christmas, and St Nick's wink too.
When I peeped round the planter and gave a soft whistle,
Away they all sailed like the down from a thistle;
But I heard them call out, as they soared through the air,
"*To all, peace and love, and a Happy New Year!*"

Three Hometown Clerihews

In Frome – his true Eden – for Adam,
life was heaven with Eve, his madam,
till Saint Aldhelm chipped in
with the notion of sin.

Beatrix Potter
never finished 'The Tale of Welshmill Sleek', Frome's
    favourite otter.
She couldn't kick her Peter Rabbit
habit.

The poet Siegfried Sassoon
wrote of life and pointless death in his platoon.
Now he rests, far from the trenches' strife and smells,
in the shade of St Andrew's, Mells.

Never
A ballad

I never see you nowadays
Life has moved on
And you are long gone
But I still dream of paradise
Together with you

I never held another hand
You were the one
We had such fun
I can't forget, please understand
Together with you

We somehow never seemed to meet
Left it to chance
Never a glimpse
But now I'm standing in the street
Together with you

I'll never let you go again
If you'll agree
I just want to be
It's really easy to explain
Together with you

Let's Call It A Day

We held hands in Paris
We flirted in Rome
We gloried in Athens
The world was our home
    If you don't want to hold me
    Don't want to stay
    Over means over
    Let's call it a day

We cuddled in Lisbon
Embraced in Madrid
We followed our lost hearts
What they felt, we did
    If you don't want to touch me
    Don't want to play
    Over means over
    Let's call it a day

Sunlight and shadows
The scent of the sea
Nightfall and daybreak
Just you and me
    If you don't want to hug me
    There's nothing to say
    Over means over
    Let's call it a day

Remember the moments
How could it not last?
But now that we're parting
It's all in the past

If you don't want to kiss me
Won't ever miss me
Over means over
Let's call it a day

Everlasting
A Frome idyll

Our eyes first crossed at the Cheese & Grain,
our hands first brushed in Zion Lane,
our lips first touched on Catherine Hill;
that was last week and I want you still.

We haunt the Black Swan from dawn to dark,
we walk and talk in Victoria Park,
it's lasted a week, it's not just a game;
surely this feeling must have a name?

Hobnob Press publishes books about West Country local and regional history, and by local authors. Find out about us and details of our publications at **www.hobnobpress.co.uk**.

Make sure you check out our **Poetry** collection

Searcher — An Almost A–Z of Poems by Judith Nicholls

The Jurassic Coast: A Poet's Journey — Amanda K Hampson

Gerontius and other poems by Pete Gage

A Celebration of Wiltshire in Poetry — Amanda Hampson

Unfrozen: Poems of the West Country — Stephen Allen

Days of Dark and Light: Recent Poems — David Thompson

Definitely Getting There — poems by Crysse Morrison

Fifty-Six Poems by Pete Gage

Stuff the Bustard and other poems — Sue Kemp

Ingram Content Group UK Ltd.
Milton Keynes UK
UKHW021815050523
421306UK00010B/127